For Paula Wiseman, great editor and friend
—R. B.

For Gavin
—R. C.

Acknowledgments
The author and publisher gratefully acknowledge the
Department of Earth and Environmental Sciences
and Lamont Geological Laboratory at Columbia University.

SIMON & SCHUSTER BOOKS FOR YOUNG READERS
An imprint of Simon & Schuster Children's Publishing Division
1230 Avenue of the Americas, New York, New York 10020
Text copyright © 2016 by Robert Burleigh
Illustrations copyright © 2016 by Raúl Colón
All rights reserved, including the right of reproduction in whole or in part in any form.
SIMON & SCHUSTER BOOKS FOR YOUNG READERS is a trademark of Simon & Schuster, Inc.
For information about special discounts for bulk purchases, please contact Simon & Schuster Special Sales
at 1-866-506-1949 or business@simonandschuster.com.
The Simon & Schuster Speakers Bureau can bring authors to your live event.
For more information or to book an event, contact the Simon & Schuster Speakers Bureau
at 1-866-248-3049 or visit our website at www.simonspeakers.com.
Book design by Laurent Linn
The text for this book is set in Arrus Std.
The illustrations for this book are rendered in watercolors, Prismacolor pencils, and lithograph pencils on Arches paper.
Manufactured in China
1023 SCP
8 10 9
Library of Congress Cataloging-in-Publication Data
Burleigh, Robert.
Solving the puzzle under the sea : Marie Tharp maps the ocean floor / Robert Burleigh ; iIllustrated by Raúl Colón.
pages cm
"A Paula Wiseman Book."
ISBN 978-1-4814-1600-9 (hardcover)
ISBN 978-1-4814-1601-6 (eBook)
1. Tharp, Marie. 2. Cartographers—United States—Biography. 3. Geomorphologists—United States—Biography.
4. Women cartographers—United States—Biography. 5. Submarine topography. I. Title.
GA407.T43B87 2016
526.092—dc23
[B]
2014010158

Solving the Puzzle Under the Sea

MARIE THARP
MAPS the
OCEAN FLOOR

Robert Burleigh

ILLUSTRATED BY
Raúl Colón

A Paula Wiseman Book
SIMON & SCHUSTER BOOKS FOR YOUNG READERS
New York   London   Toronto   Sydney   New Delhi

Maps. I *love* them!

I love the flow of colors and lines. I love the way I can trace a path with my finger across mountains or valleys until my finger has traveled thousands of miles—from here to there—on just one page.

I sometimes feel a map is talking to me. "Marie," it says. "Have an adventure. Explore. Discover something new."

And once—I did.

I'm Marie Tharp, and my love of maps began way back in the 1930s, when I was a girl. My father's job was to make maps that helped farmers understand different kinds of soil and what they could be used for. I liked to watch as Dad drew his maps. Sometimes I held his pads and pencils as he worked.

Dad traveled from state to state to make his maps—from Michigan, to Iowa, to Alabama, and beyond—and the whole family moved along with him. I had attended seventeen schools by the time I graduated high school. Try topping that!

Sometimes in class I'd gaze at a large map that hung on the wall. There was France, there was South Africa, there was China—and always the vast oceans. I had never seen a real ocean. What would it be like to look out at nothing but dark blue as far as the eye could see?

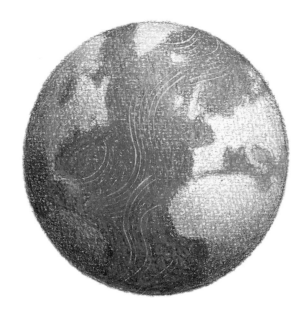

When I was in college, a teacher pointed out that though the oceans covered more than half the earth's surface, scientists knew very little about the bottom of the seas. And what did the seafloor really look like? No one seemed to know for sure.

At last I was a young scientist, graduated from college and eager to work. But was science ready for me? In those days it wasn't easy being both a woman and a scientist. Once I applied for a scientific job. They told me, "We don't need any more file clerks." Because I was a woman, they assumed the only thing I was capable of was taking care of their files!

Even at the ocean-studies lab at Columbia University in New York, my first boss—Doc Ewing—told me a woman couldn't go out on the research ships. "Having a woman on a ship is bad luck," he said. I was amazed. It was 1948. Wasn't science supposed to be free of silly superstitions?

But I bit my tongue. That wasn't going to stop me. I was determined. I took on every little task I could, helping here, assisting there. Yes, I was bored sometimes (once I even thought of quitting), but I kept on. I was looking for something that really excited me, something that might lead to a new idea in the world of science.

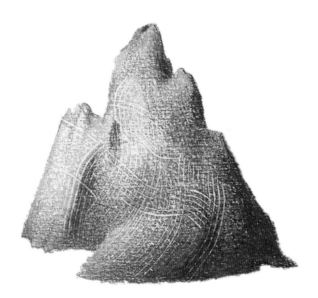

At the lab I worked hard and made lots of friends. One of those friends was Bruce Heezen, a colleague who worked with me on several projects. Both of us were interested in breaking new ground. How deep were the oceans? Were there mountains beneath the sea? Or was the bottom mostly flat?

One day we had an exciting idea. Could the seafloor really be mapped?

I thought so—and I wanted to give it a try!

People had long attempted to measure the depth of the oceans. Sailors once lowered weighted ropes to make such measurements. More recently, scientists had begun using machines that sent sound waves from a ship to the seafloor and back again. Using the time it took for the echoes to go and come bouncing back, it was possible to figure out the depth at various points.

These measurements are called "soundings." As time passed, more soundings were made, including some by my friend Bruce. And these soundings gave me my starting point.

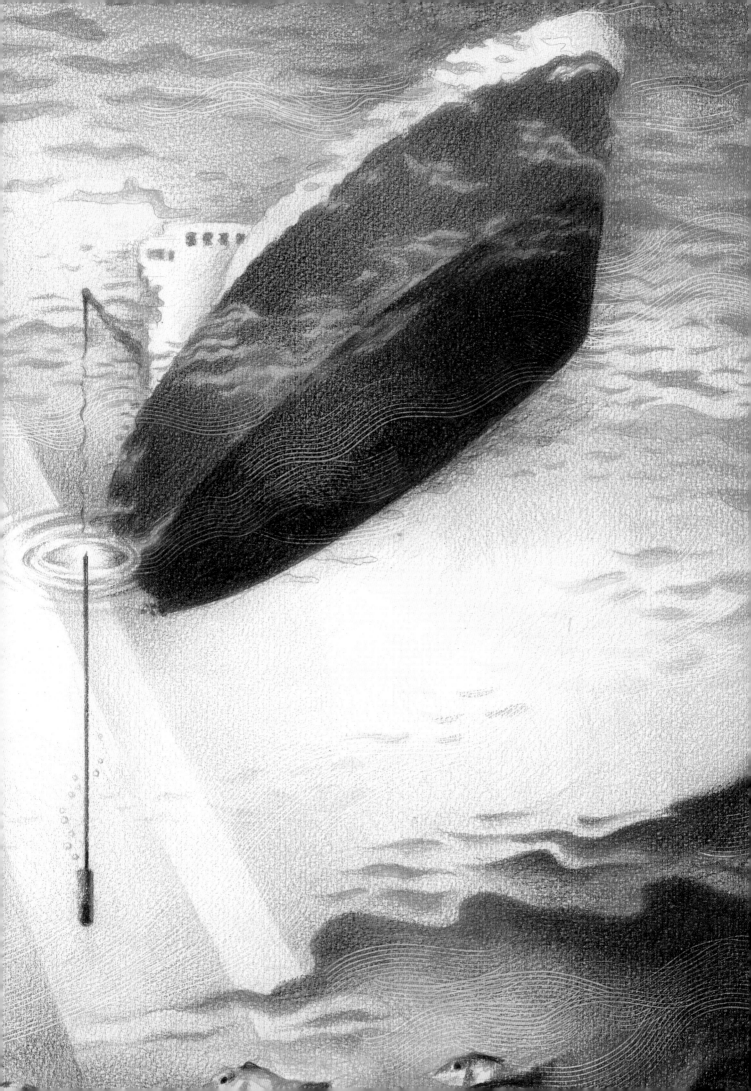

You have to think big, I told myself. I hauled a large table into my workroom and covered it with a huge sheet of paper. To me it was a blank canvas filled with possibilities. I couldn't wait to get started.

I began by drawing the coastlines—first of the Americas, then of Africa. Between these coasts lay my target: the wide Atlantic Ocean. Next I slowly collected all the soundings available and placed their numbers carefully where they belonged on my map.

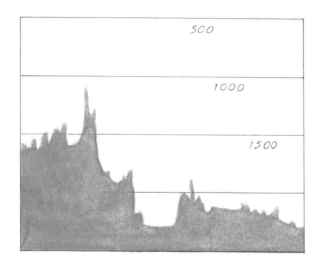

Each sounding told the ocean's depth at one point. If the sounding number was, say, 16,000 feet, it meant the ocean was 16,000 feet deep right there. And if at a nearby point the depth was, say, only 8,000 feet deep, the sudden difference between the two numbers meant there was probably a mountain-like peak rising upward. And yes, there *are* mountains beneath the ocean, just as there are on land.

It was like piecing together an immense jigsaw puzzle. I felt like a detective solving a great mystery.

I was a scientist at last. Pinpointing the soundings helped me slowly understand the shape of the Atlantic's floor: from its shallow shores, to its gradual drop-offs where the water deepened, to a long underwater mountain chain—called the Mid-Atlantic Ridge—that ran deep below the surface, north to south.

I was a kind of artist, too. I used colors to show similar depths—shades of brown, blue, and green. Did all this take time? Yes. Even so, making a scientific discovery is worth it. I couldn't see it with my eyes, yet a "portrait" of the ocean floor was coming into view.

But there was even more.

Listen.

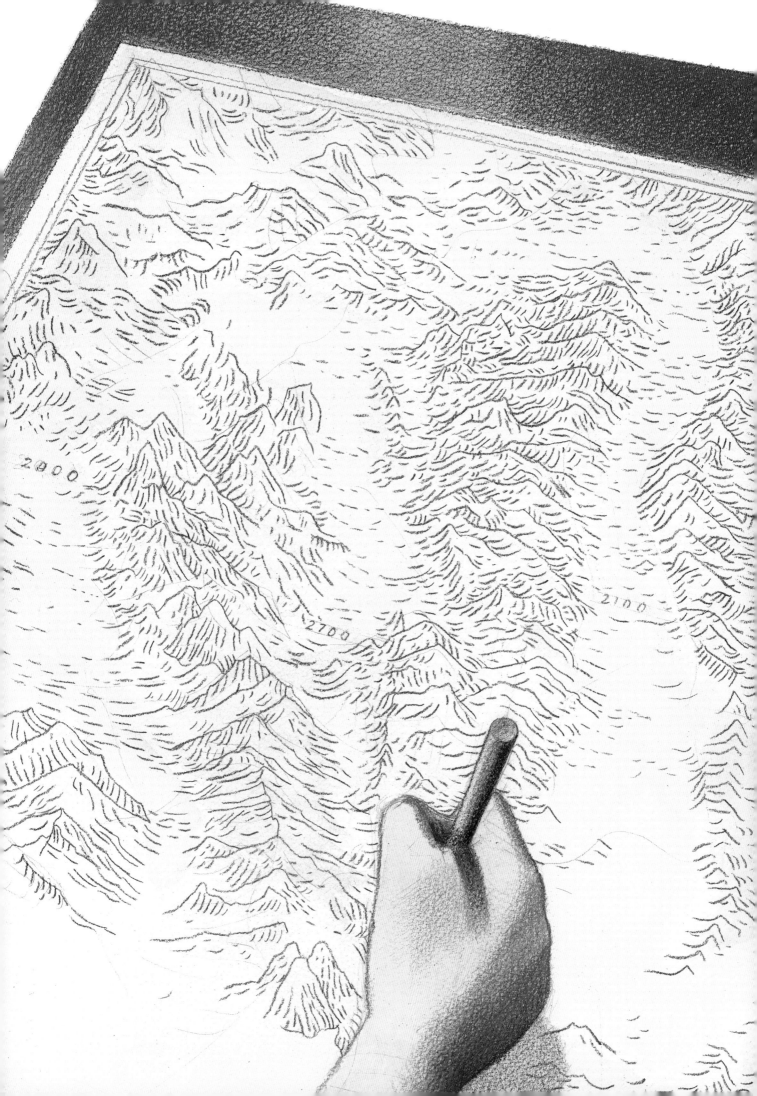

I noticed something else, something new and important. The depth numbers on my map suggested that a deeper narrow valley divided the seafloor of the mid-Atlantic into two parts.

At that time, most scientists believed the earth's surface never moved. The earth, of course, moved around the sun. Yet the earth's surface, so these scientists assumed, was fixed, unmoving.

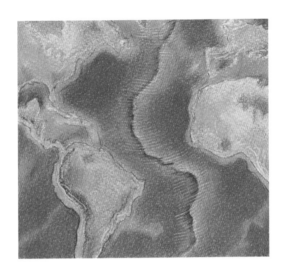

Other scientists, though, thought differently. They had an idea, or hypothesis, that the earth's entire surface was divided into several gigantic parts, or "plates." They thought these plates were being forced apart by deep-sea earthquakes and volcanoes that occurred along the plate edges. And because the continents rested on these plates and moved as they moved, the new theory was called "plate tectonics" or "continental drift."

Was the new theory true? I believed it was! My map, showing the deep crack, or rift, running between the mountain peaks of the Mid-Atlantic Ridge, was telling me so.

As I continued working, others wandered in and out of my room, arguing about continental drift. Was it true? Yes, no, yes, no. (Scientists are like that. They question everything. Nothing is for sure—until it's really for sure.)

Even my friend Bruce refused to believe the new theory at first. But I ran my finger down the map, following the narrow path of the north-south rift at the center of the Atlantic Ocean's mountain chain. I smiled to myself, remembering that a picture is worth a thousand words.

Bruce at last nodded and agreed.

It felt good. I knew we were changing the way people looked at the earth.

We asked a landscape painter from Austria to help us with our map's final printed version. I still remember the first time I saw it—with its rich colors, many markings, plains, and peaks. I felt like an explorer gazing at a newly discovered part of the world. Other people agreed, I guess, because when the map was published, it appeared in museums, in schools, and even on the walls of many homes.

Was I proud of myself? You bet. I had a fascinating job that led me to map a once unknown part of the earth and to discover things as I went along. That's about as big as it gets!

And, yes, my map helped prove that the earth's surface is moving, too. But don't worry. You won't lose your balance. We're only moving about an inch or two each year!

Marie Tharp, born in 1920 in Ypsilanti, Michigan, was one of the twentieth century's most important scientists. She was a key figure in helping to map and understand the seafloors around the world. Her work was also valuable in proving the theory of continental drift: that all the continents on earth move very slowly, toward or away from one another, over time.

Marie had a somewhat unusual childhood. Her father was a mapmaker himself, working in different parts of the United States for many years. The family moved often, and Marie eventually attended seventeen different schools before entering college. She was a curious and exceptional student: during her college years in the 1940s she received degrees in four fields: music, English, mathematics, and geology.

After working briefly for an oil company in Oklahoma, Marie moved to New York City in 1948, where she began working at the Lamont Geological Laboratory (now called the Lamont-Doherty Earth Observatory) at Columbia University.

Despite meeting some opposition (women at the time were thought to be unfit for scientific research), she slowly gained the confidence of the laboratory director and was given the project for which she became famous: mapping the bottom of the world's seas, starting with the Atlantic Ocean.

This large project, undertaken with fellow geologist Bruce Heezen, took place between 1957 and 1977. While Heezen and others collected data on many ocean trips, Marie used the information to carefully assemble it on a series of maps that revealed the shape and special features of the bottom of the Atlantic Ocean. The mapping of other oceans would soon follow.

At the same time, Marie's work led her to detect a deep crack, or rift, running along the ocean floor. The rift occurred between two underwater mountain chains. A rift is also where many earthquakes occur. This discovery helped scientists realize that the earth's surface was divided into several huge plates, which were always moving. It was used to confirm the theory of continental drift.

It took years for Marie's work and achievement to receive full recognition. In 1998 she was honored during the 100th anniversary of the Library of Congress's Geography and Map Division. The following year, the Woods Hole Oceanographic Institution recognized her, and in 2001 her home institution honored her with the Lamont-Doherty Heritage Award. Today a fellowship at Lamont-Doherty to promote women in science through the ADVANCE program bears her name.

Marie Tharp died in 2006. Among the many tributes that she received, one scientist put it very simply: "Marie didn't just make maps. She understood how the Earth works."*

*Bill Ryan, Doherty Senior Scholar, Lamont-Doherty Earth Observatory. Quoted in "Remembered, Marie Tharp, Pioneering Mapmaker of the Ocean Floor," *Columbia News* (August 24, 2006).

SOME WORDS AND PHRASES TO KNOW

cartography
the art and science of mapmaking

continental drift
the extremely slow movement of the earth's continents over time

earth scientist
a person who studies any of the earth sciences, such as geology or oceanography

geology
the science that studies rocks, mountains, plains, and other land formations to help us understand how the earth was made and how it continues to change

hypothesis
an idea about how things work that scientists think is probably true, which they attempt to prove or disprove using scientific methods

Mid-Atlantic Ridge
a tectonic plate boundary that is part of the longest mountain range in the world, beneath the Atlantic Ocean

oceanography
the science that studies all facets of the oceans

Pangaea
a supercontinent that formed about 300 million years ago and began to break apart about 200 million years ago to eventually form the continents we have today ("Pangaea" means "all lands" in ancient Greek).

plate tectonics
according to this theory in geology, the surface of the earth is divided into plates whose movement causes earthquakes and other seismic events

rift
a deep crack in the earth's crust

Ring of Fire
rifts beneath the Pacific Ocean where many earthquakes and volcanic eruptions occur

scientific theory
a principle that scientists believe to be true but which has never been proven

seafloor spreading
the separation of tectonic plates at mid-ocean ridges, caused by liquid rock spreading upward between the plates and forcing them apart

BIBLIOGRAPHY

Your school library, your local library, and the Internet have many books and articles dealing with aspects of oceanography. Here are a few.

Barton, C. *The Earth Inside and Out: Some Major Contributions to Geology in the Twentieth Century*. London: Geological Society Publications, 2002. Marie Tharp, oceanographic cartographer, and her contributions to the revolution in the Earth Sciences.

Dipper, Dr. Frances. *Secrets of the Deep*. New York: DK Publishing Company, 2003.

Felt, Hali. *Soundings*. New York: Henry Holt and Company, 2012. A wide-ranging biography of Marie Tharp, with a great deal of information, but written for adult readers.

Heezen, B. C., Hollister, C. D. *The Face of the Deep*. New York: Oxford University Press, 1971.

Jackson, Kay. *Oceans*. Mankato, MN: Capstone Press, 2006. An easy-to-read starter book on the subject of oceans.

Kalman, Bobbie. *Explore Earth's Five Oceans*. New York: Crabtree Publishing Company, 2010.

Verne, Jules. *Twenty Thousand Leagues Under the Sea*. New York: Alfred A. Knopf, 2013. A famous nineteenth-century fantasy book about undersea exploration.

INTERESTING INTERNET LINKS TO EXPLORE

National Geographic Education: http://education.nationalgeographic.com/education/activity/undersea-geology/?ar_a=1

National Oceanic and Atmospheric Administration Education Resources: http://www.education.noaa.gov

Scientific American: http://www.scientificamerican.com

Smithsonian National Museum of Natural History Ocean Portal: http://ocean.si.edu/ocean-life-ecosystems

Woods Hole Geographic Institution: http://www.woodshole.com

Do you like maps? Try mapping your route to school. Get a piece of paper, and draw your home on one side and your school on the other. Then fill in the roads and buildings you pass on your way to school. Now you're a cartographer—a maker of maps.

Read a book or Google "oceans" and try to find out how deep the world's oceans are at their deepest points. (Hint: it's over five miles!)

Try to take a few soundings of your own. If you live near a lake, go out on a small boat with your mom or dad, tie a stone to a long string, and drop the string in the water until it hits the bottom. The length of the string is the depth of the water at that point. Take a number of soundings and later see if you can make a picture or diagram of the bottom of the lake!

If magma (liquid rock) pours out of the cracks, or rifts, in the ocean floor, what do you think might be found deeper still, in the middle of the earth? (Another hint: think *very hot*.)

How do you think Marie Tharp felt when male scientists told her she couldn't go out on the boats that measured the ocean's depth? How would you feel?

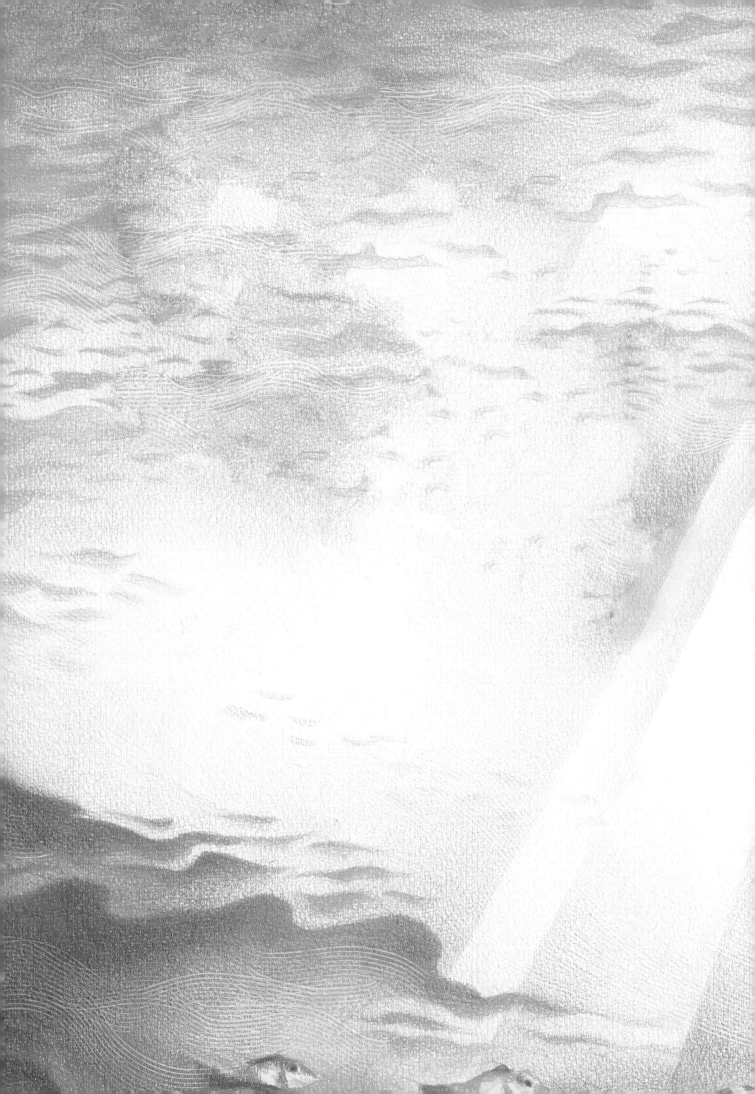